The
LIGHT
In My
ROOM

Written & Illustrated
by
William Wilkerson

ISBN: Softcover   978-1-6641-7720-8
        EBook   978-1-6641-7719-2

To order additional copies of this book, contact:
Xlibris
844-714-8691
www.Xlibris.com
Orders@Xlibris.com

Print information available on the last page

Rev. date: 05/26/2021

I dedicate this book to my Lord and Savior, Jesus Christ. You are the light of the world, and the light in my room.

To my mother, Victoria Hannans who loved all of her children and inspired each of us to be light!
To my loving grandmother, Lelia Hannans whose love was an undeniable light of love which impacted both her children and her grandchildren and all who knew her.

To my mother & father-in-law, John and Rosetta Davis, who left a legacy of love and light that will never be forgotten.
- William W.

...IN THE BEGINNING, GOD SAID LET THERE BE LIGHT!

God is light!!!

1 JOHN 1:5 (KJV) - This then is the message which we have heard of Him, and declare unto you, that GOD is light, and in Him is no darkness at all.

Psalm 119:105 (KJV)- Thy word is a lamp unto my feet, and a light unto my pathway.

Light is Truth.
Light is Love.
Light is Hope.
Light is Peace.
Light is Revelation.
Light is Spiritual
Enlightenment.

Be LIGHT!

...There are times when darkness seems to dim the light that we have within. However, if we find that there is very little light in our room, we need to make room for the light ...Seek light; Be light!

Jesus replied, "My light will shine for you just a little longer. Walk in the light while you can, so the darkness will not overtake you. Those who walk in darkness cannot see where they are going. Put your trust in the light while there is still time; then you will become children of light." John 12:35,36 (NLT)

...FOR YOU WERE SOMETIMES DARKNESS, BUT NOW ARE YOU LIGHT IN THE LORD: WALK AS CHILDREN OF LIGHT: Ephesians 5:8 (KJV)

You are the LIGHT of the world—like a city on a hilltop that cannot be hidden. No one lights a lamp and then puts it under a basket. Instead, a lamp is placed on a stand, where it gives light to everyone in the house.
Matthew 5:14,15 (NLT)

Sometimes when I look outside my bedroom window; I can see my reflection staring back at me. My truth is not my reflected image, nor is it my reality. However, it is in that reflective moment that I can see a deeper truth revealed by my LIGHT within.

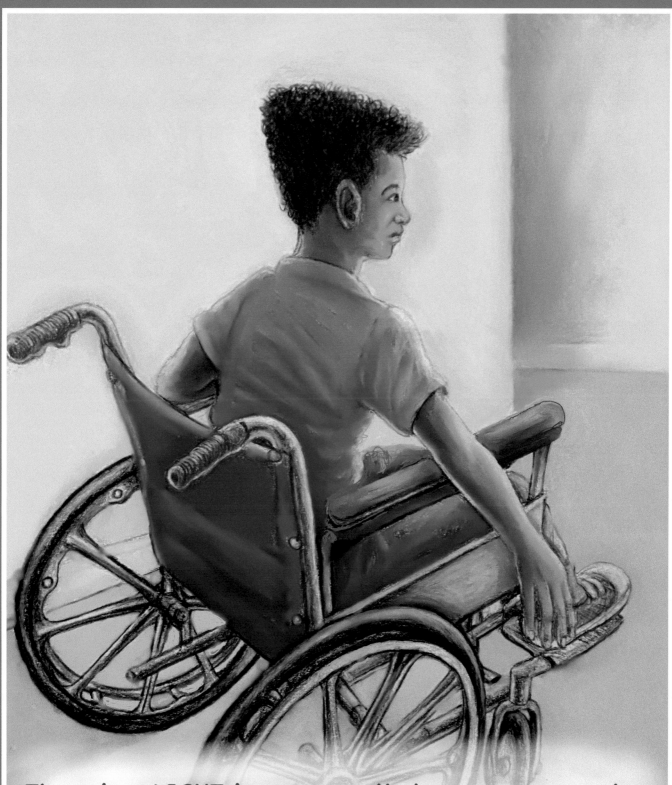

There is a LIGHT in my room that opens my eyes to all things good. My HOPE resides in HIM who is the source of all LIGHT.

The LIGHT in my room helps me see clearly in dark moments. It guides me towards an inner path that creates moments that allows me to express myself joyfully. My JOY comes from within!

My mother encourages me to believe what the BIBLE tells me about me; — I am not defined by what's on the outside, but what's on the inside. I am a child of LIGHT.

The LIGHT in my room is the light of GOD's TRUTH. God's LIGHT sets you free from the cares and darkness of this world.

LIGHT is TRUTH—..."And you will know the truth and the truth will set you free."
John 8:32 (NLT)

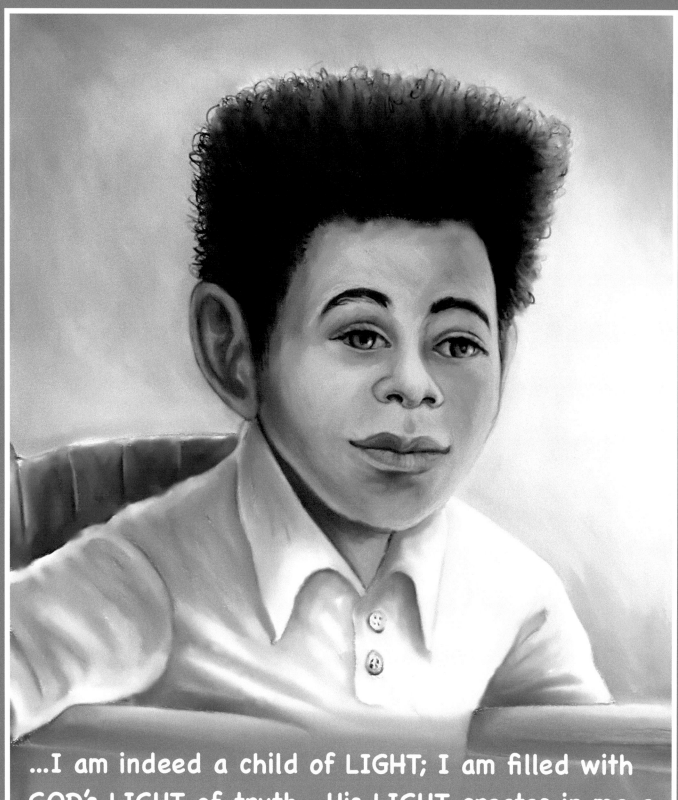

...I am indeed a child of LIGHT; I am filled with GOD's LIGHT of truth. His LIGHT creates in me a righteous attitude. Even in darkness, I will not be fearful.

The LIGHT in our room helps us see that it is important to show love and kindness to others.

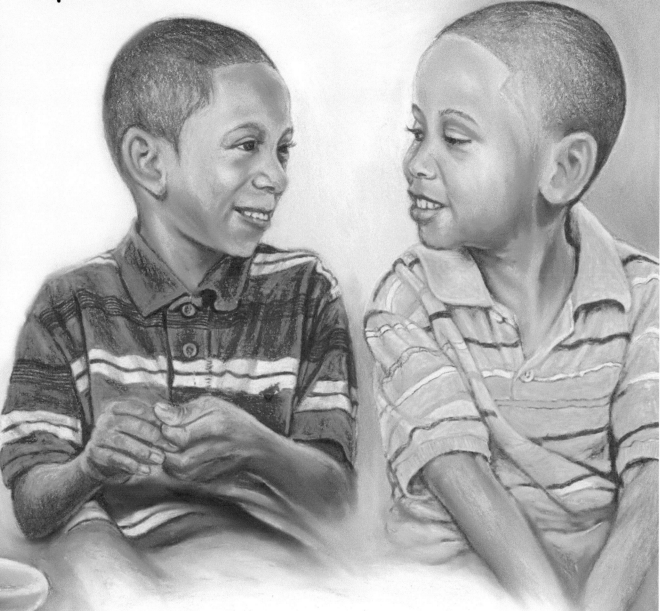

For you are all children of the LIGHT and of the day; we don't belong to darkness and night.
1 Thessalonians 5:5 (NLT)

With tender love and care, our parents and grandparents were the beacons of light that guided us through the turbulent waters of darkness. Their LIGHT steered us safely towards the PEACEFUL shores of RIGHTEOUSNESS and TRUTH.

Their Light is the legacy of love that has shown so brightly in years past, and its profound truth is still evident and still guiding even today.

Our LIGHTS are those shared and precious moments of love that we are able to spend with our family and with each other. LIGHT is LOVE without condition. We are sisters; and we are LIGHT.

The LIGHT in my room is a LIGHT of JOY and HAPPINESS. My LIGHT lets me see and discover new and wonderful things about life and myself. —I am LIGHT!

Because I am LIGHT, I will seek HIS LIGHT and TRUTH in all things.

My LIGHT is a light that shines like words on the pages of a good book; and with each sentence, new and great possibilities are revealed. Seek LIGHT!!

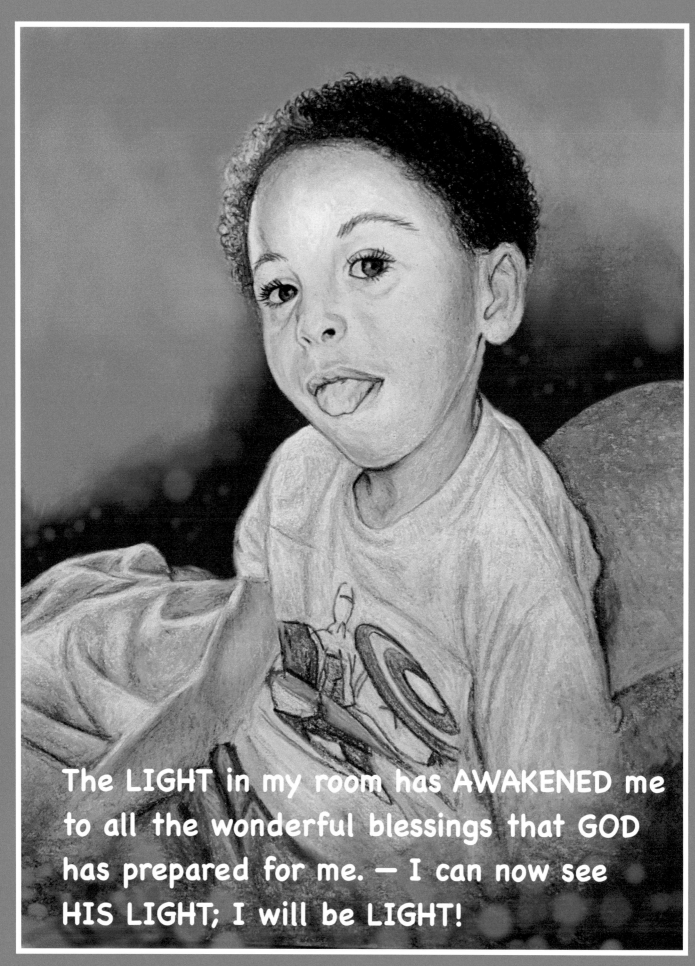

The LIGHT in my room has AWAKENED me to all the wonderful blessings that GOD has prepared for me. — I can now see HIS LIGHT; I will be LIGHT!

The **LIGHT** In my room has **shown** me the value of HUMILITY. I will continue on the path that GOD has chosen for me. I will be LIGHT!

The LIGHT in my room let's me see that JOY and ENTHUSIASM, during challenge are necessary ingredients to have in ones pursuit of TRUTH.

The LIGHT in my room shows me the value of being confident and believing in myself. Once you have found your path to enlightenment, let your light shine brightly, so that others might find their way as well. ...I am LIGHT!

For GOD, who said, "Let there be LIGHT in the darkness," has made this LIGHT shine in our hearts so we could know the glory of GOD that is seen in the face of JESUS CHRIST.

2 Corinthians 4:6 (NLT)

The LIGHT that shines in my room, is a LIGHT that shines with purity; it allows me to see a clear path which points me towards my divine destiny. I am LIGHT!

The LIGHT in my room shows me the value of being kind. I will always try to show love and kindness to others.
— KINDNESS is my LIGHT.

The LIGHT in my room is the Light of Compassion and consideration for others. I am hopeful that I can encourage others to be compassionate as well. — I would like to show GOD'S LIGHT to everyone.

THIS LITTLE LIGHT OF MINE

THIS LITTLE LIGHT OF MINE
I'M GONNA LET IT SHINE
THIS LITTLE LIGHT OF MINE
I'M GONNA LET IT SHINE
EVERY WHERE I GO,
I'M GONNA LET IT SHINE
EVERY WHERE I GO,
I'M GONNA LET IT SHINE

LET IT SHINE
LET IT SHINE

My LIGHT is like a bright and colorful sunrise at the beginning of a new day. I can feel its radiant warmth within; and the origin of its beauty is from GOD'S HOLY SPIRIT. — A SPIRIT that resides in all children of LIGHT. This little LIGHT of mine, I will let it shine for all to see.

My little LIGHT is the light in my room, and it shines everywhere I go. My little LIGHT reflects the LIGHT of GOD's SON, and its HIM I want all to know. - Show HIS LIGHT to all, and be LIGHT!

Light is the beginning of understanding. I too am a child of LIGHT, and there is a divine LIGHT inside my room.

The LIGHT in my room is the LIGHT of FAITH. I can see and dream big dreams; and if I can dream it, I can do it. My aim is set on reaching and being one of the highest and brightest stars.

Light is the beginning of many flowering possibilities...

LIGHT is like radiant smiles that rise from luminous pools of JOY that resides deep within each of us; Smiles that are like candles that can light up any situation.

My Light gives me HOPE and allows me to dream about all the wonderful and exciting possibilities that exist within me — I am determined to be LIGHT!

Seek LIGHT...Be LIGHT!

Set your affection on things above, not on things on the earth. Colossians 3:2 (KJV). ...Seek GOD's Light.

SEEK LIGHT... — BE LIGHT!

For you are the fountain of life, LIGHT by which we see.
Psalms 36:9 (NLT)

There are those whose very lives served as guiding lights for others to follow. Their light has influenced many to be champions for justice; and for those systematically marginalized by attitudes influenced by darkness. Be LIGHT!

LIGHT will forever be triumphant over darkness!
You are victorious; Celebrate the LIGHT In your
room!!

BE
LIGHT!

Printed in the United States
by Baker & Taylor Publisher Services